Ghost Hunters

WILLIAM W. LACE

THE LIBRARY OF
Ghosts & Hauntings

ReferencePoint
Press®

San Diego, CA

For more information, contact:
ReferencePoint Press, Inc.
PO Box 27779
San Diego, CA 92198
www.ReferencePointPress.com

Picture credits:
Cover: Photoshot
AP Images: 18, 33, 37, 58, 62, 66
Dreamstime: 22
IStockphoto.com: 6, 24, 27, 53
Landov: 39, 44, 49
Photoshot: 13, 15
Science Photo Library: 10, 69

Series design and book layout:
Amy Stirnkorb

LIBRARY OF CONGRESS CATALOGING-IN-PUBLICATION DATA

Lace, William W.
  Ghost hunters / by William W. Lace.
      p. cm. -- (The library of ghosts and hauntings)
  Includes bibliographical references and index.
  ISBN-13: 978-1-60152-091-3 (hardback)
  ISBN-10: 1-60152-091-3 (hardback)
  1. Ghosts. 2. Parapsychology. I. Title.
  BF1461.L155 2009
  133.1--dc22

                                                                    2009008164

Contents

The Ghostly Relative

Donald and Sarah Wrenn were puzzled—and a bit scared. Their four children were having recurring nightmares. Three of them—Karen, Jesse, and Adam—said they had seen black shadows in their rooms. The youngest, five-year-old Ellen, said she had spoken with a woman who lived in her bedroom closet.

The parents could not find a natural explanation, so they turned to the supernatural. They called Jason Hawes and Grant Wilson in Rhode Island, founders of The Atlantic Paranormal Society (TAPS) and probably the world's most famous ghost hunters.

The Wrenns' case occurred in 1997, seven years before Hawes and Grant's hit television show *Ghost Hunters* made its debut on the Sci Fi channel. The ghost-hunting team was not yet famous, but their reputation had grown enough to receive a call from the Wrenns in New Hampshire.

Modern ghost hunting can consist of hours or days waiting for something—and often nothing—to happen. This time was different. As Hawes, Wilson, and two colleagues began setting up their equipment in a hallway, they saw a dark mass. They tried to film it, but the camera battery was dead—drained of energy, Hawes thought, by a supernatural force.

A Loud Bang

Shortly afterward, a motion detector went off and a loud bang came from the girls' bedroom. Karen and Ellen were under their covers, and a closet door, which had been closed, was open. The girls went back to sleep after their mother told them that the noise was from one of the ghost hunters' cameras toppling over. An hour later, however, Karen fled from the room, screaming about the closet.

The ghost hunters investigated. "We saw that Ellen was still fast asleep, but in the recesses of the closet, a dark shape that looked like a woman was sitting on some cardboard boxes. The air in the room was oppressive—warm and thick, like the hottest summer days," Hawes wrote. When they moved closer, the figure vanished, "but not before we got a sense of its all-too-human features."[1]

When the girls' mother heard a description of the figure, she turned pale. It might, she said, be her great-aunt who had died recently and whose possessions were stored in the Wrenns' basement.

As Hawes and Wilson went down the basement stairs, they heard footsteps behind them—but no one was there. As they neared the deceased woman's belongings,

they felt themselves pushed from behind, which, Hawes notes, "was jarring to say the least."[2]

Old Clothes

Since Sarah Wrenn had said the unusual activity started about the time of her relative's death, the ghost hunters suggested she get rid of the stored items—mostly clothes—and have the house blessed by a priest. The Wrenns followed this advice, and the trouble ceased.

Altogether, it was a satisfying experience for the ghost hunters. They had, in their view, encountered a spirit and were able to put both it and the family it was haunting at rest.

Ghost hunting, however, has never been—and still is not—an easy path to follow. Skeptics scoff, and the ghosts themselves—if, indeed, there are such things— have been stubbornly unwilling to provide concrete evidence of their existence. But the hunters keep on hunting, and incontrovertible proof of ghosts would be their greatest discovery.

OPPOSITE: Creepy basement stairs may hide a ghostly presence. This appeared to be the case when ghost hunters Jason Hawes and Grant Wilson investigated strange occurrences in a New Hampshire house. Heading into the basement, the pair heard footsteps behind them but saw no one.

CHAPTER 1

Ghost Hunter History

Although ghosts—or at least those who believe in them—have been around throughout human history, people who actively hunt them are a fairly recent phenomenon. A few investigations into supposed supernatural activity took place in Europe in the 1600s and the 1700s, but paranormal investigators, or ghost hunters as they are more popularly known, date mostly from the 1920s. The roots of ghost hunting, however, stretch back to the spiritualism movement.

Spiritualism, the belief that spirits of the dead can be contacted through people called mediums, was first preached by a Swedish mystic in the 1700s, but the movement became widespread due to the activities of the Fox sisters from the tiny hamlet of Hydesville, New York.

In 1848 the Fox family moved into what was locally believed to be a haunted house where, according to local legend, an itinerant peddler had been murdered. Soon, family members began hearing mysterious knocking sounds. Kate claimed to have been touched by a cold hand while she was sleeping. Her sister Margaret said that rough fists had pulled the blankets from her bed.

Eventually, the story goes, the girls developed a system through which the knocks were translated into messages. The spirit, they told other family members and neighbors, was indeed that of the unfortunate peddler. At this point a woman who had worked in the household about the time the murder supposedly took place recalled having tripped in the basement over a small mound of newly turned dirt. When the basement was dug up at the spot she indicated, a piece of bone identified as part of a human skull was found.

The Word Spreads

Kate and Margaret became a sensation locally and later at the Rochester, New York, home of their elder sister Leah, who actively sought publicity from local newspapers. When word of their séances, meetings at which communication with spirits is supposed to take place, eventually reached showman P.T. Barnum, he brought them to New York City, where their clients included such notable people as author James Fenimore Cooper, newspaperman Horace Greeley, and poet and editor William Cullen Bryant. Many years later, in 1888, Margaret confessed that the sisters had made the sounds by cracking their big toe joints, but by that time the belief in spiritualism and the number of mediums had mushroomed.

Many of the mediums were, like the Fox sisters, frauds, and the earliest paranormal investigators were dedicated to exposing them. One such group was the Ghost Club, established in 1862 by a group of intellectuals in London. This group, whose members included novelist Charles Dickens and chemist William Crookes, challenged mediums from the United States who had come to Great Britain to perform.

Occasionally, however, people applying scientific methods to the investigation of mediums ran up against phenomena they could not explain. A small but influential group of such investigators resolved to keep their minds open to the possibility of spirits. One of them,

Did You Know?
Within Great Britain's Ghost Club, a person who dies was considered just as much a member as one still living.

William Crookes illuminates a spirit that was said to have materialized during a séance. Crookes and other London intellectuals were members of the Ghost Club, a group formed in 1862 to investigate and expose trickery among mediums.

philosopher William James, worried that science, by branding all supernatural events as fraudulent, might be ignoring "a natural kind of fact of which we do not yet know the full extent."[3]

The SPR Is Founded

Three people—poet Frederick Myers, psychologist Edmund Gurney, and philosopher Henry Sidgwick, who had been active in the Ghost Club— came together in Great Britain in 1882 to establish the Society for Psychical Research, or SPR. A sister organization was founded in the United States three years later.

Prominent members of these societies included future British prime ministers Arthur Balfour and William Gladstone; authors Arthur Conan Doyle, Mark Twain, and Lewis Carroll; and psychiatrists Sigmund Freud and Carl Jung. They published a journal, held conferences, formed committees, and conducted investigations. For the most part, they were upper-class intellectuals. They were not at all prepared for Harry Price, the first of the modern ghost hunters.

Son of a London grocer, Price became interested in the supernatural at the age of 15, trying— unsuccessfully—to photograph a spirit he heard climbing up a staircase. He was also interested in magic and became an expert magician, a skill that was to help him investigate and expose fake mediums.

Price joined the SPR in 1920 and two years later won notoriety by exposing a man named William Hope, who took photographs that, when developed, supposedly showed the spirit of deceased relatives. The next year, however, Price encountered Stella Cranshaw, whose powers of telekinesis, or moving objects without touching them, seemed to be genuine. One of Price's investigative devices was a large glass jar covering a telegraph key that operated an electric light. Cranshaw, without touching the jar in any way, seemed to be able to turn the light on.

The Schneider Brothers

Price also investigated the German mediums Willi and Rudi Schneider. Even though connected to a device that would signal any movement of their hands or feet, they seemed to be able to make objects in the room move about. His experiences with Cranshaw and the Schneider brothers convinced him that some paranormal experiences might well be genuine.

From this point on, the focus of Price's investigations changed from exposing fraudulent mediums to more serious investigations of the supernatural. However, his methods and his blatant seeking of publicity did not suit the stuffier members of the SPR, and in 1926 Price established his own organization, the National Library for Psychical Research. His work eventually became so well known that the University of London in 1934 incorporated his library into its new Department of Psychical Research. In 1938 he reestablished the Ghost Club, which had been dissolved 2 years earlier.

By this time Price had done much to turn paranormal research from a pastime for intellectuals to a popular craze. He investigated cases that the SPR would have spurned but that attracted newspaper coverage, such as a spell that supposedly would turn a mountain goat into a monkey or the case of a talking mongoose. Instead of publishing papers to be read only by society members, he wrote books with titles such as *The Haunting of Cashen's Gap*. He titled another book *Confessions of a Ghost-Hunter*, thereby coining the term.

Using the Airwaves

In addition to newspapers and books, Price publicized his work through the relatively new mass medium of radio. He was accompanied on some of his investigations by R.S. Lambert, host of a popular show called *The Listener*. He also conducted his own broadcasts from supposedly haunted houses, much to the discomfort of prim executives at the British Broadcasting Corporation. The talking mongoose case, for instance, created so much publicity that the BBC tried to dismiss Lambert, who filed suit and was able to keep his job.

Price did not restrict ghost hunting to a few privileged insiders but opened it to the public. During his most famous investigation—Borley Rectory in the English county of Essex—he ran an advertisement in the London *Times* seeking "responsible people . . . to join observers . . . of alleged haunted house. Printed instructions supplied."[4]

Price, however, was much more than a showman. He conducted investigations with such care as to set a precedent for all the serious ghost hunters who followed him. The "instructions" referred to in the advertisement made up his *Blue Book*—the first ghost hunter's guidebook. Observers were told, for instance, never to approach a mysterious form or apparition, to speak only if the apparition speaks, and to note its method of vanishing.

The Ghost Hunter's Kit

He devised the first ghost hunter's kit, which contained cameras, tape measures, flashlights, and candles. He employed the most advanced technology available, including remote-controlled cameras and devices to measure and record room temperatures.

The investigation of Borley Rectory would occupy Price off and on from 1929 until his death in 1948 and would result in two books, *The Most Haunted House in England* and *The End of Borley Rectory*. For many years, residents of the house had heard phantom footsteps and odd sounds and had seen strange lights and a mysterious figure resembling a nun. In 1938 it was reported that during a séance a ghost identified herself as having once been a nun in France. She had left her convent to marry Henry Waldegrave, whose family manor house had stood on the spot where Borley Rectory was later built.

The spirit was said to have told the researchers that Waldegrave had strangled her and buried her in the manor house cellar. Borley Rectory was mostly destroyed by fire in 1939, but one of Price's associates, a clergyman named W.J. Phythian-Adams, used this information and other clues to tell Price in 1943 where to dig in the ruins. Price found a woman's jawbone, part of a skull, and some religious medals. After the bones received a religious burial, the phantom nun was never again seen.

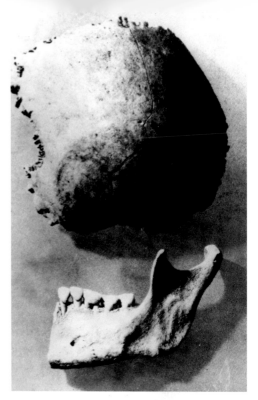

This jawbone and piece of skull, both from a woman, were found buried under Borley Rectory. After receiving a religious burial, the ghost associated with the bones has never been seen again.

By the time of Price's death in 1948, ghost hunting was an established, if not always respected, occupation. Modern author and ghost hunter Troy Taylor writes that Price "is the one person who so many modern investigators . . . emulate today with their own research. Price managed to give 'ghost hunting' a place in the public eye."[5]

Peter Underwood

Price's successors, including Peter Underwood, Hans Holzer, and Ed and Lorraine Warren, developed similar reputations. As is so often the case with ghost hunters, Underwood, born in 1923, had his first paranormal experience early in life, claiming at age nine to have seen an apparition of his father, who had died earlier in the day. Later, he lived with grandparents in a centuries-old house that was said to be haunted.

He worked with Price on the Borley Rectory case, and after Price's death became executor of, or had legal control over, Price's papers and writings. He had joined the Ghost Club at Price's invitation and served as its president from 1962 to 1993.

Underwood, like Price, made extensive use of the mass media, hosting a series of 10 television programs titled *The Ghost Man*. He has also been a prolific writer with almost 50 books to his credit. Soon after the Ghost Research Foundation was created at Oxford University in 1992 with the announced mission of studying reported haunting and paranormal events worldwide, the members invited Underwood to be their official patron and gave him the title King of the Ghost Hunters.

Hans Holzer

Underwood is rivaled in reputation and extent of publication by Holzer, born in Vienna, Austria, in 1920. Like

Borley Rectory (pictured) was described by renowned ghost hunter Harry Price as the most haunted house in England. Price spent years investigating reports of phantom footsteps, strange lights, and mysterious figures in the house and in the ruins after it burned down.

Underwood, he became interested in the paranormal at an early age and remembers reading ghost stories to his kindergarten classmates. He took a more scholarly route to ghost hunting than most practitioners, earning a doctor of philosophy degree in parapsychology, or the branch of psychology that deals with the paranormal.

Holzer is quick to correct those who say he deals in the supernatural. "There is no 'supernatural world,'" he told an interviewer. "Everything that exists is natural. Yet there is a dimension of existence that is as real as your living room, even if the average person cannot access it with all their senses."[6]

Like Underwood, Holzer is a prolific writer, but where Underwood has concentrated on Great Britain, the majority of Holzer's works deal with the United States. His 160 books include volumes on the ghosts of Washington, D.C., New York City, New England, and California.

Like Harry Price, Holzer is most often connected to a single haunting. In his case it is the famous case of a house in Amityville, New York. In 1974 Ronald DeFeo Jr. murdered 6 family members in the house. The next year George and Kathleen Lutz and their 3 children moved in. The Lutzes remained there only 28 days, driven away by such reported occurrences as green slime oozing from the walls and a piglike creature with glowing eyes.

The case was turned into a best-selling book and popular movie, *The Amityville Horror*. Holzer was one of several ghost hunters who later investigated the house, suggesting that it may have been occupied by an evil spirit because of the murders. Holzer has written three books on the case, including the novel *Murder in Amityville*, subsequently made into the film *Amityville II: The Possession*.

The Warrens

Ed and Lorraine Warren also researched and investigated the Amityville house and reached the same conclusion as Holzer. Their reputations—and Holzer's—suffered when it was widely reported, though never proved, that the Lutzes had invented the story. The Warrens also investigated the case of Jack and Janet Smurl and were convinced that the Pennsylvania couple had been assaulted by demons, even though other investigators could not corroborate their findings. Their book on the

The First Ghost Hunt

The earliest known account of a ghost hunt was by the Roman writer Pliny the Younger (A.D. 61–115). It tells of a house in Athens, Greece, that was haunted by the ghost of an elderly man who rattled chains binding his hands and feet. No one could live in the house for long, and it wound up deserted.

A philosopher, Athenodorus, bought the house at a bargain price, determined to get rid of the ghost. On his first night there he saw the phantom, rattling chains and beckoning to him. He followed it into the courtyard, where it vanished. Athenodorus marked the spot, and digging the next morning revealed a skeleton wrapped in chains. After the skeleton was given a proper burial, the ghost was never again seen.

case, *The Haunted*, was later the subject of a film.

Like so many ghost hunters, Ed Warren had had an early paranormal experience. When he was five years old, he saw in the back of a dark closet what he described as a "ghost globule" in which he saw "the face of an old lady who was not looking pleasant."[7]

Ed, who died in 2006, was a devout Roman Catholic who believed in demonic possession and styled himself a religious demonologist, someone able to exorcise, or drive out, evil spirits that have taken possession of a

Ronald DeFeo Jr. (center) is escorted out of the courthouse after a 1974 hearing. DeFeo killed six people in a house in Amityville, New York. Hans Holzer investigated and wrote about the house, which was said to be haunted by evil spirits.

person's body. Lorraine is said to be a "sensitive," much like a medium in that she supposedly can sense occupants of a spirit world. Together they established the New England Society for Psychic Research in 1952 and personally investigated more than 4,000 hauntings in 50 years of ghost hunting.

While Underwood, Holzer, and the Warrens have been the elder statesmen among ghost hunters, several other researchers have made themselves prominent parts of the next generation. Books by such practitioners as Natalie Osborne-Thomason, Jeff Belanger, and Robert Southall are part of every amateur ghost hunter's library.

Hawes and Wilson

None of the more recent paranormal investigators, however, have matched the following attracted by Jason Hawes and Grant Wilson. Unlike so many ghost hunters, Hawes had his first experience relatively late, at age 22. He had been practicing Reiki, the Japanese healing technique that involves a person's "life force," when he began to have visions. "Usually it started out with a mist, out of which emanated a dim light," he wrote, "and then out of the light came other things—including see-through animals and full-body apparitions."[8]

Shortly afterward, he started the Rhode Island Paranormal Society, which began attracting like-minded believers in ghosts and other paranormal occurrences. One of these was Grant Wilson, and in 1991 the pair founded TAPS.

Wilson brought a wealth of technological experience to the group, and TAPS places a heavy reliance on high-tech devices such as electromagnetic field (EMF) scanners and ion generators. The publicity generated by their investigations eventually led to the debut of *Ghost Hunters* on the Sci Fi channel in 2004. The show produced high ratings and as of early 2009 was in its fourth season with more than 80 episodes having been telecast.

Thanks largely to Hawes and Wilson, interest in ghost hunting has never been so high. Investigators may now rely on techniques that Harry Price could have never dreamed of, but—like Price—they still are fascinated by the idea that ghosts are with us. And, as were those who have gone before them, they are dedicated to finding them.

Did You Know?
When Ed and Lorraine Warren first started hunting ghosts, Ed would sketch old houses and show ghosts coming out of them. Lorraine would give the sketch to the residents, who would usually invite them in.

What, Where, When

Hunting for ghosts, say those who practice it, is no different from hunting for anything else. You have to know what you are looking for, and you must have at least some idea of where it might be found. And in the case of things as elusive and unpredictable as ghosts, a notion of when they might appear is helpful, as well.

Almost every ghost hunter has his or her own definition of "ghosts." The classical concept of ghosts is that they are spirits of deceased persons, which for some reason remain on Earth or at least halfway between our world and some other. However, writes Troy Taylor, "many parapsychologists refuse to take [this idea] seriously."[9] They claim, he says, that some places thought to be haunted cannot be connected to a person or to a tragic event.

Taylor, however, agrees with the classical view, defining a ghost as "the personality of an individual who has once lived and has stayed behind in our world."[10] Exactly why some personalities remain while others do not is unclear. According to Hans Holzer,

> The death is not smooth. When there is trauma [such as an automobile accident] this will, in some cases, cause the personality to go into a state of psychotic shock. In that

state of shock they are not aware that they've passed on. They are confused as to their real status, because they can see everybody and nobody seems to be able to see them. That's what a ghost is . . . somebody who's gotten stuck in the physical world but is not part of the physical world. [11]

Such ghosts are referred to by such terms as discarnate, or "unfleshed," souls and disembodied spirits. According to Holzer and others, they attract attention any way they can, such as by making sounds or moving objects. Sometimes they are said to have communicated with the living through mysterious writings on walls or by spelling out messages through a Ouija board or some other device it can manipulate to spell words. Others have supposedly found their voices through mediums.

Strange Sounds

Most ghost hunters, however, report having seen or heard such spirits. Holzer tells of a case in which a woman and her daughter began to hear strange sounds in their apartment—a thud followed by a noise as if something was being moved across the floor.

The woman questioned her landlady, who said the apartment previously had been occupied by a woman and her 19-year-old son, a gifted athlete. One day, after learning he would have to have a leg amputated because of a disease, the son shot himself, fell, and then tried to make his way to his mother before he died. The mother soon moved from the apartment and died shortly thereafter.

The new tenant, however, had had some experience with the supernatural. The next time she heard the sounds, she called the young man by name and told him

Ghost hunters say that disembodied spirits sometimes use tools such as a Ouija board (pictured) to communicate with the living. The board allows them to spell out messages.

that his mother "has gone ahead of you and is waiting for you; do not keep her waiting any longer." This continued night after night until finally she heard a far-away voice say, "Mama—help me."[12] Eventually, the sounds ceased, and the woman was convinced she had put the boy's ghost to rest.

Such cases, however, are in the minority. Many more reported hauntings are "residual"—an incident in the past being replayed. It is as if, writes Taylor, an event "imprints itself on the atmosphere of the place."[13]

Ghostly Beings

In 2002 Hawes and Wilson investigated a case in which family members reported seeing ghostly beings that seemed to be moving across a room or down a staircase even though their lower bodies or feet seemed to be buried. The ghost hunters discovered that a different house had been on the spot, built on a lower level. The ghosts, they concluded, were still "walking in the paths they had always walked, unaware that a second house had replaced their own."[14]

Other kinds of hauntings, however, are thought to involve the living instead of the dead. Sometimes activity such as loud noises, furniture that moves by itself, dishes spilling out of cabinets and crashing to the floor cannot be connected with any past event or person, but rather is blamed on a poltergeist.

Poltergeists—the German word for "noisy ghosts"—seem to take their power from living people. In many cases, writes Taylor, the "human agent," often a teenage girl entering puberty, projects bursts of energy that cause loud and destructive activity. The theory is that the combination of hormonal changes occurring in the body and the resulting sexual turbulence in the brain somehow boils over into physical activity. The person often does not realize he or she is the cause of the disturbance.

The most famous poltergeist case involved a young woman in Illinois named Wanet McNeill. After her parents' bitter divorce, she and her father moved to a relative's farm. Shortly thereafter, fires—hundreds of them, small and large—broke out. Brown spots appeared on walls and ceilings, grew, and then burst into flame. The official explanation was that Wanet had started the fires with matches, but no one could explain the blazes that began when she was not present.

Two-Part Phenomenon

As usual, those within the ghost hunting community disagree about poltergeists. Some think destructive activity by a ghost and energy created by a human agent are entirely different occurrences. Others, such as Fiona Broome, contend that poltergeists are "a two-part

Did You Know?
Ghosts appear in four of William Shakespeare's plays: Julius Caesar, Hamlet, Richard III, and Macbeth.

phenomenon. The energy for the activity is provided by someone who is very much alive. The pranks and noises are caused by the ghost."[15]

Most ghost hunters agree, however, that another classification of ghosts has no human origination. Richard Southall calls them "entities" and writes that "they are completely spiritual or ethereal in nature and actually have never lived as human beings."[16] Angels are in this category, as are demons.

Ghost hunters have little experience with angels. Such encounters tend to be regarded as private by those who experience them, and the encounter is almost uni-

Because they are the final resting places of the dead, cemeteries are often associated with hauntings. The strong emotions of grieving families and friends may provide a powerful attraction for ghosts.

formly positive. Demons, however, are another matter. Most ghost hunters contend that ghosts—the kind in residual hauntings or that are between worlds—are not evil, although some are mischievous. But demons are thought to be pure evil—the exact opposite of angels—and actively seek to harm humans with whom they come in contact.

Many religions, including Christianity, have long believed that it is possible for a demon to possess a living person. The New Testament of the Bible refers to Jesus as casting out demons, and the Roman Catholic Church has retained the rite of exorcism to cure demonic possession.

Ghost hunters contend that involuntary possession is rare. Instead, Southall writes, demons are usually encountered after "an individual or individuals invite one into their lives in one fashion or another."[17] Inexperienced people conducting a séance, for instance, might unwittingly call forth the wrong kind of spirit.

The Life Force

While angels and demons belong in the realm of religion, other types of ghosts or spirits have in common the idea that people—indeed, all living things—have an energy, a life force, that acts in mysterious ways when they are alive and that continues to exist after death. This force, ghost hunters say, can manifest itself physically—in slamming doors, mysterious lights, changes in temperature, odd smells—or translate itself into humanlike forms that may be seen. In other words, the life force, once freed of the body, becomes a ghost.

Given such a wide variety of paranormal entities, it should come as no surprise that they can be found almost anywhere—or so the ghost hunters say. Nevertheless, the concept that ghosts are attracted to and feed on energy makes some spots more likely candidates than others for those who seek them.

The best-known ghost hunters, of course, do not need to seek out promising locations. Rather, the locations come to them by way of people who think they are being haunted and who turn to professionals for help. Still, they offer tips for amateurs.

Since many ghosts are thought to be the spirits of deceased persons, Belanger writes, it is logical to look for them in places where people have died or that are associated with death. Foremost among these are cemeteries, which are not only places where the deceased have been buried but are also sites of strong emotions enacted on an almost daily basis as survivors grieve over their loved ones. In addition, many people—consciously or not—have a fear of the dead, and such fears may be heightened in cemeteries, making them more receptive to supernatural forces.

The Catacombs of Paris

Belanger had his own experience in such a place. In 2003, during a visit to France, he visited the catacombs, a network of tunnels under the city of Paris. The tunnels were originally dug to get limestone for building construction, but between 1785 and 1859, when the graveyards of Paris had no more room, the remains of more than 6 million people were brought below and packed into tunnels, which were then sealed off.

Walking through the tunnels, Belanger came to an arch over which was written, in French, "Stop! This is the Empire of the Dead."[18] Beyond, he found pile upon pile of bones, including skulls staring back at him. Moments later he began seeing shadows darting quickly across the tun-

A network of supposedly haunted tunnels known as the catacombs (pictured) lies beneath Paris. The remains of millions of people were packed into the tunnels (inset) when the city's graveyards filled up between 1785 and 1859.

nel. "I was the only living thing down there big enough to cause a shadow that large, and I know my shadow was safely at my feet," he writes. "I was in the place of the dead, I was alone, and that's what I saw."[19]

Not everyone agrees that cemeteries are prime locations for ghosts, contending that spirits are far more likely to frequent places where they lived or died rather than where they were buried. "How many people do you know that have actually died in a graveyard?" asks Wilson. "Not many."[20]

Cemeteries, however, are not the only places of the dead. Ghosts have been reported at many battlefields, where visitors tell of hearing horses' hooves, faint bugle calls, and the sound of distant gunfire. In his article on the Civil War battlefield at Chickamauga in Tennessee, Dale Kacsmarek of Ghostresearch.org relates several such reports.

Old Green Eyes

One Chickamauga story deals with an apparition known as Old Green Eyes, which one local legend claims is the ghost of a decapitated soldier who roams the site, moaning mournfully while looking for his lost head. Even though headless, Green Eyes seems to have eyes. Park ranger Edward Tinney once saw him walking along a trail and described him as having greenish orange eyes and fanglike teeth.

Other places thought likely to be haunted are those with a history of human misery, such as hospitals and prisons. Southall investigated one such site, Moundsville Penitentiary in West Virginia. Many sightings of ghosts had occurred there, both before and after it was closed in 1995. One was said to be that of R.D. Walls, a prisoner brutally murdered in the 1930s by fellow inmates.

The Spookiest Cemetery

One of the most haunted cemeteries in the United States, according to the Travel Channel's Web site, is the St. Louis Cemetery on Basin Street in New Orleans, Louisiana. Tombs and mausoleums containing the remains of more than 100,000 persons are built aboveground because of the marshy ground.

The most famous resident ghost is said to be that of Marie Leveau, a voodoo queen who died in 1881. Those who claim to have seen her say she walks between the tombs wearing a red and white turban while loudly mumbling voodoo curses at trespassers.

While Southall and some other ghost hunters were in the room where Walls's body had been found, Southall thought he heard the person next to him say, "Right here."[21] The person denied having said anything. Then, when Southall tried to take a photograph of the scene, his camera would not work, even though the batteries were fully charged. When he left the room, the camera worked perfectly.

But while ghosts have been encountered in various kinds of locations, most ghostly experiences take place in homes. The plots of countless stories and films revolve around haunted houses, but what makes a house haunted?

Houses with Histories

Age can make a difference, ghost hunters say, not because the house is simply old, but because it probably has been lived in by generations of people, each contributing their own experiences and life energies. It also helps if the house has a "history"—if a violent death or suicide took place there.

Holzer writes about one such house in Oklahoma, near an army base. In 1971 it was rented by a family consisting of a soldier, his wife, and their young son. After about 2 weeks, the wife began to hear soft footsteps in the hall. When she investigated, no one was there. One day she heard the sound of a child crying. Her own son was playing happily in the back yard, so she traced the crying to her own bedroom. When she entered, the crying stopped. Eventually, she learned that 2 years earlier a previous tenant had beaten his 2-year-old daughter to death. The crime had occurred in the room from which the crying seemed to come.

A house does not necessarily have to fit the classic picture—the spooky old mansion on a lonely hill—to be considered haunted. One of Hawes and Wilson's early cases took them to a high-rise apartment building in Toronto, Canada. The owner reported that doors had been opening and closing on their own, and furniture had mysteriously moved. In one apartment a box of golf balls was seen to empty itself on the floor with the balls arranged in the shape of an arrow.

Did You Know?
According to ghost hunter Hans Holzer, ghosts most often appear at night because the quieter, less distracting atmosphere makes it easier for them to communicate with the material world.

Apartment 10-C

The ghost hunters finally narrowed the center of the paranormal activity to apartment 10-C, whose tenant had recently been evicted for nonpayment of rent. The former resident had been a student of the occult, and the apartment was full of mysterious symbols. Hawes and Wilson concluded that the evicted man had, before he left, somehow allowed a demonic spirit to enter. Under the guidance of a priest, the entire building was blessed with holy water, ending with 10-C. As the ceremony progressed, dishes began flying from the kitchen cabinets and smashing on the floor. Suddenly, the activity stopped. All was quiet. The demon, they felt, had departed.

Much of the paranormal activity recorded by ghost hunters has occurred in broad daylight, and experts have different ideas on the optimum time to look for ghostly activity. Valerie Hope and Maurice Townsend, editors of *The Paranormal Investigator's Handbook*, recommend night because the lack of distractions makes apparitions easier to see. Patricia Telesco writes that "ghosts are more readily seen at midnight and on the anniversary of their death."[22]

Broome herself inclines toward what she calls the "between times"—dawn and dusk—and the changing of the seasons. "Perhaps a door opens between worlds when conditions are slightly unstable,"[23] she writes.

The goal of ghost hunters is not to capture a ghost or necessarily to eliminate it. Rather it is to try to find evidence that ghosts exist. Like any scientist seeking after the unknown, ghost hunters are more likely to be successful if armed with the knowledge of what they are after and the best conditions for making the discovery.

Did You Know?
Abandoned buildings or houses that appear to be in a good state of repair are cited as likely spots for ghosts, since the owners might not otherwise have had a reason to leave.

High-Tech Ghost Hunting

In 1937 Harry Price's *Blue Book* set forth a list of essential equipment for the would-be ghost hunter. The basics included a flashlight, candle and matches, notebook and pencil, sandwiches and brandy, and rubber- or felt-soled shoes. If the hunter had a camera, fine, but that was about the extent of technology. Ghost hunting was primarily a matter of watching and waiting.

In the intervening decades, ghost hunters have increasingly come to rely on electronic gizmos to back up, or in some cases substitute for, what their own senses tell them. It can be an expensive undertaking, but the fancy equipment has produced some remarkable results.

One of the basic tools in the modern ghost hunter's kit is the electromagnetic field (EMF) meter. Spirits are thought to have an "aura," a surrounding of electromagnetic energy. Some investigators think ghosts depend on such energy for their existence and can feed on other energy sources, draining a camera battery, for instance.

The EMF meter is a hand-held device that registers fluctuations in electromagnetic fields. Such fields are found in all homes, emanating from appliances, light fixtures, breaker boxes, and other sources of electricity. Most such readings are in the range of 9.0 to 30.0 Hertz depending on the amount of electricity and the proxim-

A paranormal investigations expert demonstrates the use of a video camera and an electromagnetic field meter at a Wisconsin cemetery. The electromagnetic field meter is used to detect electromagnetic energy that is thought to surround spirits.

ity of the meter to the source. Jason Hawes and Grant Wilson once thought they had found an exceptional paranormal field, a reading of 53.4, in the McGregor Room of the Stanley Hotel in Estes Park, Colorado, the place where the film *The Shining*, based on Stephen King's horror novel, was made. It turned out, however, that just beneath the room's floor was a large cable junction serving the entire hotel.

Paranormal EMF readings are generally thought to be lower than most—in a range of 2.0 to 7.0. One of the first things a ghost hunter does in an investigation is to tour the entire site with an EMF meter, recording all the readings in order to get "baseline" data. Then, any other readings that cannot be attributed to a known source may be attributable to a ghost.

The Case of Grandma's Ring

Hawes and Wilson relate how an EMF meter played a part in one of their cases, that of a four-year-old girl who claimed to have been speaking with her deceased grandmother. The ghost hunters and the girl's parents gathered in the child's bedroom, and another member of the team tried to summon the spirit by tapping together two stones considered to be sacred.

Abruptly, the temperature in the room fell by several degrees. "Our EMF meters were showing marked fluctuations in the room's magnetic field," Hawes wrote, "adding credence to the idea there was a supernatural presence among us."[24]

The child seemed to be having a conversation with the spirit and then suddenly walked out of the room and down to the basement, where she dug into a large cardboard box and pulled out a small wooden box. She handed it to her mother and said, "Grandma wants her ring."[25] The box, indeed, held the dead woman's ring, which was eventually buried next to her coffin. The spirit never reappeared.

The drop in temperature is thought to be another sign of paranormal activity, as ghosts draw energy from the heat in a room and create a "cold spot." Modern ghost hunters have a device to record such phenomena. Infrared thermometers record temperatures without having to be in contact with an object. They work somewhat like a pistol. Point it at an object, such as a wall, and sensors measure the infrared "heat signature" of the object. Many models can operate from as far away as 100 feet, although the surface area being measured increases with distance. Some come with attachments that allow the operator to measure the "ambient" temperature, or the temperature in the immediate area.

Voices of the Dead

Frequently, however, ghosts are thought to make themselves known in ways much more direct than temperature or electromagnetic fluctuations. Many people claim to have heard the voices of the dead speaking to them. Others have heard noises that seem to defy description, but which seem to come from somewhere other than the natural world. Ghost hunters have long attempted to record such occurrences, which in the world of paranormal investigation are called electronic voice phenomena, or EVP.

Many spiritualists claimed to be able to call forth the voices of the dead, but the first person to make a serious attempt to record such communication was Thomas Edison, the man who invented sound recording. Though not religious in the usual sense, Edison believed that when a person died, his or her spirit remained for a time before passing on to another existence. He was convinced he could build a device to communicate with such spirits.

Edison was never able to complete his spirit recorder. One of his friends claimed to have seen an early version, but after the inventor's death in 1931 no trace of such a device could be found. Over the next 20 years various claims of ghost recordings were made, but it was not until 1959 that EVP began to become a part of paranormal research.

In that year Fredrich Jurgenson, an ardent birdwatcher, was using a reel-to-reel tape recorder to capture the sounds of birds in the woods of his native Sweden. When he reviewed the tape, he found that he had recorded bits and pieces of human speech, although he had been alone at the time. The voices were in different languages and spoke much more rapidly. Jurgenson said he recognized one of the voices as that of his dead father.

Four years and hundreds of recordings later, Jurgenson published a book, *Voices from the Universe*. He contended that recording devices can pick up not only the sounds audible to the human ear but also those that are not. He wrote that spirits are able to use the electronic devices as a link to amplify their own voices that, on their own, are too faint to hear unaided. In 1971 one of Jurgenson's students, Konstantine Raudive, published his own book *Breakthrough*, accompanied by phonograph records.

Doubts About EVP

Some experts, Troy Taylor for one, doubt the value of EVP as evidence of ghosts, saying that too often people's imaginations take over and they hear only what they want to hear. He tells of the time that his team recorded a low, eerie moan or groan that seemed to be saying "hello." Taylor thought it had been a ghost voice and subsequently replayed it in front of a large group. As it turned out, however, the team member sitting closest to the sensitive microphone had recently eaten dinner. The sound was that of his stomach rumbling and gurgling. "Boy, was my face red!"[26] Taylor confesses.

Richard Southall, however, is a firm believer in EVP and has been since the day he and a friend investigated a farmhouse where a little girl had died in the 1880s. Before taking a lunch break, they left a tape recorder in what they thought to be a "cold spot." When they reviewed the tape, they could clearly hear a cough and then a childish voice crying for her mother. "Since that day," Southall admits, "I have *always* used a cassette recorder in my investigations."[27]

Most ghost hunting groups use technical tools in tandem. Such was the case with the Hoosier State

An infrared thermometer (pictured) helps ghost hunters search for "cold spots"—places that have an unexplained drop in temperature. An undefined red mist rising from a tool case suggests a ghostly presence.

Paranormal researchers in January 2009 when they investigated a reportedly haunted book in the library of DePauw University in Greencastle, Indiana. The book, *The Poems of Ossian, The Son of Fingal*, had been part of a collection donated to the university in the early 1800s by Governor James Whitcomb. Later the same century, a boy sneaked the book out of the library and took it home to read. After going to bed, he awoke to see a ghostly finger pointing toward him and heard a voice saying, "Who stole Ossian?"[28]

The investigators, using infrared thermometers, measured repeated fluctuations in temperature, and a digital audio recorder picked up what sounded like a man saying "I've been dead" and "I'll be back."[29]

Ghost Photography

If the reliability of ghostly voices is doubtful, then what about pictures? After all, people say that seeing is believing. However, this is not necessarily the case. The spiritualism movement produced many photographer mediums whose portraits of the living seemed to include dead relatives. Most were found to be frauds, the most famous of which, William Hope, was exposed by Harry Price.

Hope had claimed to be able to take photographs of clients in which images of their deceased relatives would appear. He did this by using a photographic plate that had already been used to take a picture of the relative. The double exposure, then, would show both the client and relative. Price provided his own photographic plate for the test, then caught Hope when he tried to substitute another.

Nevertheless, ghost hunters have continued to try to capture spirits and other paranormal activity on film.

An Ohio investigator sits in a darkened room with a tape recorder, hoping to catch ghostly voices and sounds known as electronic voice phenomena. Some ghost hunters favor this technique, while others doubt its value.

As with sound recordings, however, results have been controversial. Numerous amateur hunters swear they have photographed ghostly activity even when what appears in their pictures is shown to be otherwise. As Taylor states, "It boils down to the point that some people have such a fragile belief system that they would rather not know something than to be confronted with the truth."[30]

Paranormal photographs are also like sound recordings in that they sometimes seem to capture what the eye cannot see in addition to what is normally visible. One theory is that the camera freezes a moment in time when paranormal activity occurs, a moment passing so quickly that the human brain cannot register it. Also, some say, ghosts and spirits exist at a wavelength of light invisible to the naked eye but that can make an impression on film.

Vortices, Apparitions, and Orbs

Most of these images fall into three categories—vortices, apparitions, and orbs. Vortices are thought to be fields of paranormal energy. They may appear as streaks across a photograph or a mist or cloud. Some can be simply explained as a finger in front of the camera lens, a hanging camera strap, smoke from a cigarette, or frost from the photographer's breath.

Apparitions are the rarest form of paranormal photograph and seem to capture the figure of a ghost, including faces and sometimes clothing. One of the most famous was taken by Captain Keith Tracy aboard the SS *Watertown* in 1925. Two crewmen, James Courtney and Michael Meehan, had been killed in an accident, and some of their comrades later reported seeing their faces in the waves alongside the ship. One of Tracy's pictures clearly showed what appeared to be faces, which were later identified by relatives of the dead sailors.

Orbs are by far the most common images and the ones that also yield readily to natural explanations. Orbs are balls, globes, or shapeless globs of light that sometimes appear on photographs but were unseen by the photographer. Most have occurred when taken at night or in the dark with the use of flash photography. The light

Talking to the Dead

For more than a century the Ouija board has been one of the most popular methods of trying to communicate with the spirits of the dead. Something resembling a writing device for ghosts was known in China about 1200 B.C., and the Greek philosopher Pythagoras is supposed to have used a moving table in 540 B.C. The modern Ouija board, however, dates to 1890 when Elijah Bond, Charles Kennard, and William Maupin took out a patent on a device consisting of a planchette, or wooden pointer, that moved across a board bearing the letters of the alphabet.

Kennard is said to have called the board "Ouija" because he was told, during a séance, that the word is Egyptian for "good luck," even though it is not. In 1901 Ouija manufacture was taken over by William Fulk, a Kennard employee, who claimed he had invented the board and named it by combining the *oui* and *ja*, the French and German words for "yes." In 1966 the business was sold to the game company Parker Brothers, which still holds the registered trademark.

from the flash tends to reflect off objects such as a drop of water, a passing insect, or a speck of dust on the camera lens.

Some photographs of orbs, however, are not so easily explained. Sometimes a photograph of a person who supposedly possesses psychic powers will show the person surrounded by mysterious balls of light. Other pictures may show orbs in motion in a direction opposite from that of any wind and sometimes moving up, whereas a drop of rain or a dust mote would tend to fall toward the earth.

These orbs, leading ghost hunters say, are perhaps bursts of paranormal energy, but not necessarily ghosts. "Despite what you may see and hear, though," notes Taylor, "there is absolutely no hard evidence whatsoever to suggest that orbs are in any way related to ghosts. . . . These photos do show a type of paranormal phenomena, but just what type that is remains to be seen."[31]

Digital Cameras

Photographs purporting to show orbs increased in frequency with the development of digital cameras but have decreased as such cameras advanced in technology. The problem seemed to be that the early digital cameras—the ones in the 2.0 to 3.0 megapixel range—did not work well in low light. The photographic image did not fill in properly, leaving areas of white or colored light. Another problem with digital cameras in the eyes of some ghost hunters is that the images are fairly easy to alter with the aid of digital imaging computer software. It is possible, using such software, to add a ghostly image to a photograph. With conventional cameras the original negative could be provided as proof that no tampering had taken place.

Modern digital cameras, however, have overcome both shortcomings. More sophisticated models—those of 5.0 megapixels or higher—do not have the same problems in low light. In fact, some models have a setting enabling a photograph to be taken in virtually no light at all. In addition, these cameras can record the conditions under which the photograph was taken, and any doctoring of the picture will be reflected in this data.

In addition to still cameras, videotape and digital "camcorder" devices have found a place in the ghost hunter's bag. The sophisticated investigative team will position several such cameras in different locations and run cables to a set of monitors whereby all the locations can be watched simultaneously.

Problems with Videotape

Earlier videotape cameras shared the same drawback as the first digital cameras. They did not perform well in the dark. Recent advancements, however, enable video to be taken in low light or in no light. The newer cameras can provide infrared light that will pick up reflected heat energy in much the same way as an infrared thermometer and is the same technology used in night-vision goggles.

This thermal imaging camera provided one of the high points in the careers of Hawes and Wilson. They had just acquired one in 2005 when they were called on to investigate the Crescent Hotel in Eureka Springs, Arkansas. In the 1930s a self-styled doctor bought the hotel and turned it into a hospital for cancer patients. His supposed cures were bogus, and many patients died.

Hawes and Wilson were using the camera to scan the

Did You Know?
Ghost hunter Gina Lanier puts the electromagnetic field (EMF) detector at the top of her list of top 10 ghost hunting tools. Second is a thermal scanner; third, a digital sound recorder.

Using a camera, an Ohio investigator tries to capture an orb on film. Orbs are balls of light that mysteriously appear in photographs. Ghost hunters say orbs may be connected to paranormal activity but they do not necessarily have a link to ghosts.

basement room known as the "morgue" when Wilson spotted something. He played back the image for Hawes, who comments, "It was clearly and unmistakably the figure of a man rendered in gaudy thermal colors, less than six feet from Grant and the camera. And the figure was looking back at Grant, as if it was as curious about him as we were about it."[32]

Ultimately, the team was unable to identify who or what the figure was, but they were thrilled just the same. "We had stumbled on a full-body apparition," Hawes writes, "the Holy Grail of the ghost hunting field!"[33]

Many other items are available for ghost hunting. Some are as low-tech as dowsing rods—L-shaped rods of brass or copper held in each hand that supposedly will cross at a point where paranormal activity is taking place. Others are as sophisticated as sensors that will pick up any movement in a room or area—a far cry from Price's time when a motion sensor might consist of a string attached to a bell.

Counting the Cost

Modern ghost hunting is not an inexpensive proposition. Online ghost hunting equipment stores show electromagnetic field meters running from $32 to $174. A dual infrared/ambient air thermometer is $98. A good digital sound recorder with external microphone and earphones is about $83. Digital cameras of sufficient complexity run anywhere from $200 to $500, but a high-end infrared video camera can be around $1,000. Throw in a good flashlight for $15 and a motion detector for $30, and the total bill for the up-to-date ghost hunter is between $1,500 and $2,000.

The fancy equipment, however, is only as good as the people operating it. Ghost hunting, if done properly, requires patience, knowledge, and meticulous concern for details. As David Betz of TAPS notes, "The most valuable, obvious and, in my opinion, understated piece of equipment in any investigator's toolbox is unquestionably the investigator. . . . What you feel, who you are and what you believe will ultimately play a major role as you progress; and it is my firm belief that to listen to yourself, first and foremost, will keep you planted firmly on the path to becoming a credible investigator."[34]

CHAPTER 4

The Hunt

Once armed with knowledge and equipment, it's time to set out on a ghost hunt . . . or is it? Days or even weeks of painstaking research are often necessary before the actual hunt gets under way. Such preparation is a critical part of any investigation, but once the essential facts have been gathered, the time comes to stop studying and start hunting.

Research for a ghost hunt—hoping to find ghosts at a site where no activity has been reported—can be different from research for a ghost investigation—trying to document ghosts at a site known for being haunted. If a ghost hunt is the objective, the research begins with seeking a place that might be haunted.

One of the first places ghost hunters look is in their local library. Most good-sized libraries have local history collections, and such books can turn up information on localities that might yield paranormal activity.

Another good source, especially for more recent cases, is the local newspaper. Stories of odd occurrences or strange sightings pop up now and then, especially around Halloween, and can provide clues to a promising site. Back issues of newspapers can provide similar information, and searching has been made much easier than before with Internet search engines.

Such incidents, even if they are not reported to the

news media, are frequently reported to the police. Troy Taylor and other ghost hunters often get tips from the local police. "Police officers and investigators can be very useful to you and even fill you in on small details in the case, but only if you handle it correctly," he warns. "You have to be able to convince them that you have a scientific interest in the case and that you aren't some kind of 'nut.'"[35]

Hunt vs. Investigation

Once a likely spot has been identified, either through such digging or as the result of a call for assistance from someone who suspects they are haunted, much more research is needed but may well take place at different stages of the process. Before a ghost *hunt*, most authorities agree, the investigator should try to find out everything possible about the location before actually visiting it. If, however, it is a ghost *investigation*, such research may best be done after the site is thoroughly checked out.

It is important, according to professional ghost hunters, to enter a supposedly haunted site with an open mind. The danger otherwise, they say, is a tendency to interpret what they see in light of what they expect to see. "For instance, if you read that a little girl was killed in the home 100 years ago, you'll subconsciously have that little girl in the back of your mind, and it will taint your investigation," states Grant Wilson. "This forces you to be true to your feelings, therefore being true to the homeowner."[36]

Figures at the Altar

Ghost hunter Richard Senate relates an incident where after-the-fact research served to explain something he had witnessed. While visiting a restored Spanish mission near Lompoc, California, he saw, close to the altar rail,

Did You Know?
The Genesee County Home in Bethany was the first historical site in New York state to open its premises to overnight ghost hunts.

three small human figures. They were ragged, dirty, and when one of them turned toward Senate, he could see that its face was covered with red sores.

When Senate subsequently researched the history of the mission, he discovered that in the 1820s smallpox had killed many Native Americans served by the church. It was not, he writes, his imagination: "If I had imagined it why would I not have conjured up something that resembled the stereotypical image of the Missions of old California? Why would I have imaged the faces of the Natives marred by pox?"[37]

The techniques of site research are the same, however, regardless of whether it is done on the front or back end. One of the first steps is to interview any people who say they have witnessed the haunting, such as the owners of a house. This is, of course, much easier when the owners have already reported a haunting and are seeking help. Otherwise, the best bet is to make the first contact by a letter or a telephone call. "Showing up on their doorstep with your 'ghost hunter's kit' is not recommended,"[38] advises Taylor.

The witnesses—all family members in a haunted house, for instance—are interviewed separately if possible so all can give their own interpretation of events. All interviews are recorded and transcribed for future reference. In addition to asking directly about paranormal events, the ghost hunter, as tactfully as possible, inquires about family background, including religious or supernatural beliefs and whether the family has been under any stress.

Searching the Records

If the house has a ghostly history, the chances are that the haunting may have begun before the current residents lived there. A search of public records at the local courthouse can furnish the names of previous owners who might be able to provide more information. Hans Holzer's research came in handy when he was investigating a church near Pittsburgh, Pennsylvania, where a ghostly figure standing at the altar had been reported. The assistant pastor was reluctant to discuss the matter but finally admitted that the pastor had, indeed, seen such an apparition.

Holzer eventually asked if another building had ever been on the site. When the clergyman denied it, Holzer revealed that his own research showed that a different church building had been on the site in the 1800s. The assistant pastor then acknowledged the previous building and told Holzer some things he had not discovered—that the old church had burned to the ground and that its pastor had been a Father Ranzinger.

Historical records found in local courthouses can provide ghost hunters with crucial information about haunted sites. Experienced ghost hunters often begin their investigations by searching historical records.

"Father Ranzinger's beloved wooden church went up in flames, it appeared," Holzer writes, "and the fifteen years he had spent with his flock must have accumulated an emotional backlog of great strength and attachment. Was it not conceivable that Father Ranzinger's attachment to the building was transferred to the [present church] as soon as it was finished?"[39]

Asking Around

Talking to longtime residents of the neighborhood can be helpful, as well. Richard Southall once found that one of the best ways to find out about ghostly activity in an area is simply to ask around. Parkersburg, West Virginia, had a reputation for haunting, and Southall teamed with author Susan Sheppard to do research in preparation for a ghost tour. After doing library research on the historical background of the town, they placed advertisements in local publications seeking tales of ghosts. "Within days, the calls started pouring in,"[40] Southall reports. Within months, the tour was bringing more than two thousand people each year to Parkersburg.

Possibly the site being researched was once occupied by some other house or building. Here, again, legal records can provide the data. Such records include surveys done when the land in question was first developed and plat maps that are normally made when land is subdivided into blocks and individual lots.

The process is much the same for a building other than a residence—a business, for example—but is different in the case of something like a cemetery. Researching a cemetery can take much more time than researching a house or building. After all, dozens or even hundreds of people are buried there. In one way, however, the job is easier because all the "residents" are easily identifiable

Did You Know?
Despite many reports by former inmates and guards at the former Alcatraz prison in San Francisco Bay, no ghost hunts have ever been conducted there.

through gravestones and other markers.

The most important facts furnished by cemetery markers are the name of the deceased and the date of death. With this information, obituaries or death notices in local newspapers are easy to find. These may or may not list the cause of death, but newspaper articles at about the same time are likely to report whether the death was unnatural, such as by accident or homicide.

If the death was anything but natural, other sources of information may be available, such as the record of an examination by a coroner or medical examiner leading to a formal inquest. Such records are normally open to the public.

Getting Permission

After all the research is completed, most ghost hunters insist on taking at least two more steps before the actual observation phase begins. The first is to make sure permission to visit the site has been granted and that police or security officers are aware of what will take place. Benjamin Radford of *Skeptical Inquirer* magazine tells of a trio of ghost hunters who broke into an abandoned hospital for a nighttime investigation. They had not noticed the police station across the street from the hospital, but the police had noticed them. They were arrested and fined.

Second, since most observations will be at night, the ghost hunter normally will visit the site in the daytime to get a clear idea of the geographical layout. In a house or other building, this would include knowing the general layout as well as where hallways, stairs, closets, and such are located. A cemetery usually will have been visited to collect data, but another visit might be necessary to get an idea of what pathways lead where, and what might be tripped over in the dark.

Another important step, notes David Betz of TAPS, is to make sure that all members of an investigative team know their roles and are comfortable with them. A ghost hunt can go awry, he cautions, when an investigator tries to take on too much. "We all know that we have limits," he writes, "limits in our physical abilities and in our mental capacity. . . . A group that understands its strengths and weaknesses will invariably go far. But the realization of these limitations must start from the individual members."[41]

Mental Preparation

Finally, once ghost hunters have prepared everything else, they prepare themselves mentally for the task ahead. The members of the ghost hunting team—and the professionals emphasize that no hunt should ever be taken alone—may employ many forms of mental preparation. Fiona Broome suggests clearing the mind to help enhance psychic skills. Some investigators, she says, take a hot shower to relax. Others may listen to music or take a long walk. She also recommends a "psychic warm-up" using Tarot cards, for example.

A more conventional approach to achieving mental calmness might be a prayer or blessing, either individually or as a group. This need not be religious in nature, notes Dave Juliano, and not everyone might feel a need, but it is something that all members of a team can do to put themselves in a positive frame of mind. "I do encourage everyone to take the 10 seconds this takes and do this," states Juliano. "What can it hurt?"[42]

After entering the site, the ghost hunters' first chore is to set up the equipment. The amount of equipment varies with the group's technical know-how and budget.

Ghost hunters must be mentally prepared before they begin an investigation. One ghost hunter suggests using Tarot cards (pictured) to sharpen psychic skills before an investigation.

Experienced professionals such as Hawes and Wilson may have a vanload of expensive, high-tech equipment, but such is not always necessary for a good investigation. "Don't get blinded by the equipment you see us using on the show," cautions Wilson. "All you really need to get started is a camcorder with nightshot or infrared. . . . An audio recorder of any type will help, too."[43]

However much equipment is used, it pays to have it in good working order and tested beforehand to make certain. Extra batteries are a must, as are extra film and audio and video cassettes.

Photography Rules

When the time comes to take photographs, most ghost hunters operate under a few simple rules. One is to take care that nothing—such the photographer's finger—gets in front of the lens. Many a supposed paranormal anomaly has turned out to be nothing more than a stray camera strap.

Another rule is never to smoke. "If you can say with confidence every time that no one was smoking or had been smoking," asserts Wilson, "you rule out 98 percent of skeptics' excuses for 'mist' type pictures."[44]

Modern and Ancient

While some ghost hunters rely on high-tech methods and others prefer more traditional forms of investigation, others are comfortable using a combination of approaches—new or old—that seem to fit the occasion. Richard Senate conducted such a hunt in 2006 at an inn in Ventura, California, reportedly haunted by a ghost named Sylvia.

Accompanied by his wife, Debbie, and two volunteer couples, he started by using an electromagnetic scanner

Danger, but Not from Ghosts

Ghost hunting can be a hazardous vocation—though not necessarily because of the ghosts themselves. Veteran ghost hunters say on-the-job injuries caused by ghosts are rare. Less rare are injuries caused by living people. Seventeen-year-old Rachel Barezinski of Columbus, Ohio, was ghost hunting with some friends in August 2006 when they went onto the property of Allen Davis, whose house was supposed to be haunted. They had taken only a few steps before they retreated, got into a car, and began circling the block. Feeling threatened, Davis fired a shot at the car and hit Barezinski in the head. She made a complete recovery. Davis was arrested and sentenced to 19 years in prison for felonious assault.

in the inn's reading room. The device, normally used to see if appliances such as microwave ovens are leaking radiation, is sometimes used to detect any energy fields thought to be put out by ghosts. As he scanned the room, Senate was surprised at one spot to see the needle that indicates radiation level leap into the dial's red zone, indicating a potentially dangerous amount of energy. Furthermore, the zone of energy seemed to move, and the lights began to flicker. "My skin was crawling," Senate writes, "because of ghosts or my own reaction to the readings, I don't know."[45]

Senate then turned to a much older method of detecting energy—dowsing rods—for the volunteer hunters to try. In short order, the rods, held loosely in each hand, crossed at the same point where the high energy level was detected.

Then, it was again time for a more modern tool—a digital camera. One picture showed, on the shirt of one of the volunteers, a triangular light. Senate worked out a simple code to communicate with the spirit, which indeed turned out to be Sylvia, who said she had been murdered in the inn 60 years before.

From the new, Senate then returned to the more traditional, conducting a séance. Instead of Sylvia, more spirits were heard from, according to Senate, including one named Lawrence, who turned out to be the father of one of the volunteer hunters. "It was a night I shall not forget in a long time," he writes. "The data with the scientific tools confirmed something that shouldn't have been there, and the information gathered with the rods and during the séance experiment gave new information to follow up."[46]

Using One's Senses

Broome contends that a good ghost hunt can be conducted with no equipment at all except the ghost hunter's own senses. "You should be able to show up at a place that's haunted and *sense* the ghosts," she states. "The more often you go on ghost hunts, the more sensitive you'll become to ghosts and the paranormal. It's that simple. Any of the five senses can be involved, or it may be just a 'sixth sense' encounter with the other side."[47]

Did You Know?
According to the Shadowlands Web site, California has 30 ghost hunting groups, which is more than any other state in the United States.

Once everything and everyone are in place, ghost hunting is primarily a matter of watching and waiting . . . and waiting . . . and waiting. Most of the time, nothing much will happen. In fact, a string of entire nights can go by without anything at all happening. "Boredom can be an investigation killer," Betz writes. "For any enthusiastic investigator, [long periods of inactivity] will be one of the most challenging issues to work through."[48]

The Traveling Table

When things do happen, however, they can happen fast. Holzer was once conducting an investigation in the New York townhouse belonging to actress June Havoc when a table began to move violently on its own. Holzer and his team had been touching it lightly, letting it bounce on its own, tapping out a message.

Suddenly, Holzer recalls, "the table became very excited . . . and practically leapt from beneath our hands. We were required to follow it to keep up the contact, as it careened wildly through the room. . . . Eventually, it became so wild, at times entirely off the floor, that it slipped from our light touch and, as the power was broken, instantly rolled into a corner—just another table with no life of its own."[49]

At such times, seasoned ghost hunters try to keep calm. "Panic is another emotion to keep in check" advises Al Tyas of the Washington, D.C., Metro Area Ghost Watchers. "Everyone gets scared, and it's justified. [But] the worst thing you can do is let out a blood curdling scream in a suburban neighborhood at 2 A.M. . . . Just imagine the reaction of the neighbors, the police, fire department and the client when a circus forms on the front of their front lawn all due to one investigator with unsteady nerves."[50]

With dowsing rod in hand, an investigator prepares to search for signs of ghosts on a haunted railroad bridge in Vermont. The dowsing rod, better known as a tool for finding underground water, is also used to detect energy that might be associated with ghosts.

Some experts, Fiona Broome among them, claim that ghosts cannot harm the living. Demonic spirits may be harmful if they take possession of a living person, she asserts, and a poltergeist's activity may cause some bruising, but a true ghost—the spirit of one formerly living—usually has powers "significantly less than an average living person's."[51]

The Armory Ghost

The members of TAPS might not totally agree. During a 2004 investigation of an armory in Massachusetts, they were checking out an area of cold spots when their camera battery began losing power at an abnormal rate. Then, without warning, the feet of sound technician Frank DeAngelis flew out from under him, and he land-ed hard on his back. Moments later, crying and badly shaken, he described to Hawes what had happened. "It had begun with a feeling of extreme cold," Hawes relates. "Then he'd felt something come up through the core of his body and yank his head back." The incident, Hawes continues, was "the most violent documentation of the supernatural that either Grant or I had ever seen."[52] DeAngelis never went on another ghost hunt.

If someone is injured or is very badly frightened, the best thing for them to do may be to leave. "Ghosts do not follow you home," says Broome. "If you are frightened and leave a haunted location, the spirits generally do *not* go with you and they *cannot* affect your thoughts. If you are troubled by unwanted thoughts . . . relax. Eat some comfort food. Watch a happy movie or TV show."[53] Another solution is to keep busy with the work that is usually left to do after all the observations have been made and the equipment packed away. All events are meticulously documented, and all recordings examined. It may mean many hours of listening to tapes or watching a video monitor, but countless instances of paranormal activity have shown up only on recording devices, even though investigators were in the room when it happened. And, while remote cameras are helpful in that they are able to record events when no one is present, their drawback is that someone must review them.

From beginning to end, the success of a ghost hunt depends on the patience, skill, precision, and attitude of the investigator. "It is imperative that [the ghost hunter] uses his mind, judgment and his powers of observation to the utmost of his ability," states Taylor. "There are no cameras or fancy gadgets that can take the place of a good investigator."[54]

Science or Pseudoscience?

Although a national survey in 2005 showed that 73 percent of Americans believe in paranormal events, a good many are outspoken in their disbelief. One of them, James Randi, is so confident that the paranormal cannot be proved that he has a standing offer of $1 million to anyone who can prove that the supernatural exists. Dozens of people each year accept Randi's challenge. None has walked away with the money.

Randi, once a professional magician who went by the name of The Amazing Randi, retired in 1988 and began a second career investigating and exposing people who fraudulently claim psychic powers. He began his challenge with $1,000 of his own money. Donations to his James Randi Educational Foundation have swelled the amount to $1 million.

More than 150 people have claimed to be able to do everything from talking telepathically with animals to projecting 3-D images onto a piece of foil by staring at it. What they have to do to win the money, according to Randi, is easy. "All they have to do is what they say they can do," he said. "It's that simple. They have to define what they can do, and it has to match the description of being paranormal, or occult, or supernatural—that's a problem they all have. They can't define it. They can't say what they can do, under what circumstances, so they negotiate literally for years."[55]

And yet, despite the absence of concrete proof of ghosts, interest in them is high. One reason may be the growing number and popularity of ghost hunting books and television programs. In the 2005 survey, nearly 70 percent of respondents said they watch *Ghost Hunters* on a regular basis. Indeed, the exploits of Hawes, Wilson, and their associates seem to have spawned numerous imitators. "Ghost hunting groups are proliferating all over the United States,"[56] says Joe Nickell.

Nickell should know. As a senior researcher for the Center for Inquiry, his job is to investigate supernatural claims for the magazine *Skeptical Inquirer*. And he is one of the skeptics whose numbers have increased along with ghost hunters.

Skeptics vs. Debunkers

Skeptics are sometimes called "debunkers," exposing the bunk, or fraud, behind supernatural claims. But Randi claims they are different. He defines a skeptic as "someone who doubts in the absence of evidence. A debunker is someone who goes into a situation with the attitude that 'This isn't so, and I'm going to prove it to be not so.' That's why I don't accept the term 'debunker' to define myself."[57]

Several ghost hunters agree with Randi. Asked if he believes in ghosts, Hans Holzer replied,

> I don't believe in anything. Belief is the uncritical acceptance of something you can't prove. I work on evidence. I either know or I don't know. There are three dirty words in my vocabulary: belief, disbelief and supernatural. They don't exist. There's no

Did You Know?
The late psychologist Robert A. Baker, who thought ghosts were figments of the imagination, was famous for saying, "There are no haunted places, only haunted people."

Once a professional magician and escape artist known as The Amazing Randi, James Randi is now an investigator of paranormal and pseudo-scientific claims. He has offered $1 million to anyone who can prove the existence of the supernatural.

"supernatural world." Everything that exists is natural. Yet there is a dimension of existence that is as real as your living room, even if the average person cannot access it with all their senses.[58]

And Cody Polston of the Southwest Ghost Hunters Association writes that a true skeptic "holds beliefs tentatively and is open to new evidence and rational arguments about those beliefs."[59]

But all too often, skeptics say, ghost hunter groups are made up of people who have strong beliefs in the existence of ghosts. Such people go into an investigation with a preconceived notion of what they hope to find. But, according to Randi, hoping for a result is not the same as expecting one.

> I'm prejudiced against it [the supernatural] from experience—from knowledge of the subject. I can't possibly claim that I'm not prejudiced against the phenomenon being true because I've been with it for many, many years. I've seen hundreds of people who tried to prove their claims, and none of them have been able to prove it. That doesn't prove that there is no such thing, it just shows that I have a prejudice based on experience.[60]

Information, Not Conclusion

The problem with many ghost hunters, in the skeptics' view, is that they conclude that an event is paranormal if a natural explanation cannot be found. Ghost hunters and skeptics do not just come to different conclusions, states Alison Smith, one of Randi's associates. "I view the same information [as the ghost hunter] and come to no conclusion at all. There is only information."[61]

And so, the skeptics say, ghost hunters cannot possibly arrive at a valid conclusion as to whether a person is psychic or a phenomenon has been caused by a ghost.

Did You Know?
One paranormal Web site lists 384 ghost hunting groups from Massachusetts to Malaysia.

Why? "They work off the assumption that ghosts and psychics are proven phenomena," writes Smith. "They are not. Never before has there been indisputable evidence that there are psychics or ghosts."[62]

Those who claim that what cannot be explained must be paranormal, writes Nickell, are guilty of "a logical fallacy called arguing from ignorance. . . . One cannot draw a conclusion from lack of knowledge. Besides, an event may not be unexplainable at all, only *unexplained*, possibly later being solved."[63]

"Very Little Fact"

Ghost hunters sometimes counter criticism by saying that science does not have all the answers. Wilson admits that "there is very little fact in this field. . . . Face it, you can't recreate this stuff in a lab, yet."[64] And Belanger claims that some skeptics are as closed-minded in one direction as believers are in the other. "This group of people must also operate under the assumption that science is finished—that today we know everything there is to know about the universe," he writes. "This is a ridiculous position to take, of course, because science makes discoveries all the time that make old ideas moot. . . . True science is a quest for knowledge wherever it may lead."[65]

Smith agrees—to a point. But she says that science must draw conclusions based upon a rigorous method of observation and experimentation in light of natural laws as understood at the time. "It is true that supposed 'laws of nature' change," she writes. "Though it would seem that this means science is just as fallible [imperfect] as belief, in truth we are just always growing in our capabilities—scientifically and observationally—and we have to revise our truths based on that. It does not mean that the original law was unfounded, only that its

Did You Know?
Professor Michael Persinger of Laurentian University, Canada, has suggested that changes in geomagnetic fields caused by tectonic stresses in the Earth's crust or solar activity could stimulate the brain's temporal lobes and lead to sightings of what are taken to be ghosts.

application is not universal."[66]

Skeptics say that investigations done by many ghost hunters who claim to be scientific do not follow the scientific method—observation, followed by a hypothesis or proposition to explain the observation, experimentation, analysis of data, and conclusion. Such investigations, says Don Riefler, founder of a skeptics group at Purdue University in Indiana, are thus flawed from the very start. "They work from a system of assumptions, none of which have any proof of veracity [truth]," he argues, "and pawn off what they do as 'scientific' even though their very 'science' presupposed some sort of soul and 'life after death.'"[67]

Such ghost hunters also may—consciously or not—eliminate or tend to distrust any findings or data that do not fit in with preconceived notions. At the same time, findings that seem to support those notions may be accepted without rigorous checking. As retired psychology professor Robert Todd Carroll puts it, "If one is selective enough, one can confirm just about any hypothesis."[68]

Pseudoscience

Those ghost hunters who rely on mediums or clairvoyants open themselves up to another criticism, says Polston. "You cannot use the paranormal to prove the paranormal," he writes. "Simply put, this is a circular argument [since] not one single experiment in modern research has ever been able to conclusively prove the psychical talents of these so called mediums."[69]

What ghost hunters are frequently practicing, skeptics assert, is pseudoscience, or "false" science. "They typically have no scientists, and while they're using some scientific equipment, they're not trained in using the

A medium in central Florida advertises her services. Mediums say they can help people communicate with spirits, but skeptics criticize ghost hunters who rely on mediums for connecting with ghosts.

scientific equipment and they don't know what they're doing,"[70] says Nickell.

Polston calls this type of investigative technique "fringe or alternative science" and says that those who practice it are "almost always individuals who are not in contact with mainstream science." They try to explain phenomena with vague terms. "Phrases such as 'energy vibrations' or 'subtle energy fields' may sound impressive," Polston concludes, "but they are essentially meaningless."[71]

Polston adds that ghost hunters who engage in pseudoscience frequently cite other ghost hunters or groups as the authority for what they present. Riefler calls this a "feedback loop" in which each person's "faith in the methods is reinforced by the faith of another ghost

A Logical Look at Ghosts

In addition to the lack of proof that ghosts exist, says Benjamin Radford of *Skeptical Inquirer* magazine, some of the suppositions about ghosts defy logic. In an article for *Live Science* magazine he notes that if victims of unsolved murders are likely to become ghosts, many more ghosts would be reported. Citing statistics that only 64 percent of the approximately 30,000 homicides in the United States in 2002 were solved, he asks, "Where are all the ghosts? And why aren't they helping to bring their killers to justice, with so many crimes unsolved? Why would they hang out in scary mansions instead of directing police to evidence that would avenge their murders?"

Benjamin Radford, "Reality Check: Ghost Hunters and 'Ghost Detectors,'" Committee for Skeptical Inquiry. www.csicop.org.

hunter and vice-versa. 'This works because Bob says so,' says William, and Bob believes because William does. They all use the same methods, none of which has any claim to actual reliability or proof."[72]

The Technology Controversy

No aspect of modern ghost hunting draws the scorn of skeptics as much as the equipment, how it is used, and what it supposedly shows. Nickell suggests that the popularity of *Ghostbusters*, a 1984 movie in which the heroes use nuclear accelerators that fire proton streams that neutralize the a ghost's energy, may have started the equipment craze. But while they may have fancy gadgets, he says, the typical ghost hunter is "a nonscientist using equipment for a purpose for which it was not made and has not been shown to be effective."[73]

Electromagnetic field detectors, for instance, measure alternating current—the kind used in homes and businesses. The current that occurs naturally in living beings—and might, by extension, be expected to occur in ghosts—is direct current that is not detectible by an EMF detector.

Other kinds of equipment, such as infrared thermometers and Geiger counters, for example, may be more accurate, but they measure only what they were made to measure—temperature and radiation. They cannot measure supernatural activity, skeptics say, because no such thing has been shown to exist. "If [ghost hunters] get a reading on their EFM meter," says Nickell, "or if they get a picture of an orb on their camera—and because they don't know what's causing that—they say, 'Therefore it must be a ghost.'. . . They're ghost buffs, they're enthusiasts and yes, they read stuff off the Internet, but they're not trained. You don't want people

A scientist measures the electromagnetic field created by electrical devices at a cement plant. Electromagnetic field detectors have established uses in industry. Skeptics say these devices are misused by people searching for ghosts.

just reading the occasional medical article and going to practice medicine."[74]

Technology Defended

Ghost hunter Vince Wilson defends the use of high-tech equipment. "What makes us think that an EMF meter can even detect a ghost?" he asks.

> Well, for one thing, we don't think that. EMF meters, IR thermometers, barometers, and so on—what are they exactly? What were they designed for originally? Why, detecting environmental conditions, of course!
>
> We are not looking for ghosts directly, but their effects on existing environmental conditions. There is one fundamental, unbreakable law in this universe. You [or a ghost]

cannot enter an environment without changing that environment. That's what we base our research on.[75]

Ghost hunting falls into the category of pseudo-science, according to Carroll, because real science has either not been used or has failed to prove the existence of anything supernatural. "[Ghost hunters] arrive with . . . devices that were not designed to detect ghosts and therefore have no instructions on how to use them for that purpose," he maintains. "The equipment looks scientific, but does that make the investigation scientific? I'd say you're about as likely to detect a ghost with a Sony camcorder as you are to get the truth out of a house plant by hooking it up to a polygraph [lie detector]."[76]

But whether it's because of their van full of equipment, the popularity of their *Ghost Hunters* television program, or the influence they've had on the spread of ghost hunting, the skeptics seem to reserve their most severe scorn for Hawes and Wilson. Nickell, a bit more charitable than most, says "they're the best of a bad lot. . . . But I'm afraid that what I said about ghost hunters in general is true of them as well."[77]

SAPS vs. TAPS

The strongest criticism of TAPS, however, comes from Alison Smith. At first she found the presentation convincing but then began looking closer. "I soon began to notice inconsistencies," she reports. "Sometimes the group's members would say things that were patently false."[78] For instance, she continues, in one episode a ghost hunter said that the movement of a chair across a room, apparently on its own, could not have been done with fishing line since the line would show up on nightshot camera. Smith and three friends experimented for themselves and found that, indeed, fishing line could have been used as well as black thread.

Shortly afterward, she and three friends began what they call the Skeptical Analysis of the Paranormal Society (SAPS), recording and analyzing television programs on the paranormal. Smith writes that they have yet to find any proof that paranormal activity exists.

What bothers Smith as much as what the ghost hunters present is the way it is presented. She notes that TAPS uses a technique resembling what psychologists term false memory implantation. Often, she says, Hawes, Wilson, and their colleagues will talk excitedly about a phenomenon that has been filmed before actually showing it, thus preparing the viewer to interpret it in a certain way. They then "immediately shut down any possibility that the experience wasn't paranormal at all by making a statement that sounds like fact but, in actuality, isn't."[79] She cites the comment about the fishing line and chair as an example.

Hawes and Wilson claim not to be bothered by such criticism. "We're not trying to prove anything to the skeptics," said Wilson. "We try to help people who think their homes are haunted." And Hawes adds, "All a skeptic is is someone who hasn't had an experience yet."[80]

And so, despite the skeptics, ghost hunters keep pursuing their quest. Some, such as M.J. Henion, dismiss the criticism. "If they want to make a mockery of it, let them,"[81] she writes. Besides, they can take comfort in knowing that, even though no one has proved conclusively that ghosts do exist, no one has conclusively proved that they do not. The next house, the next graveyard, they can hope, might just provide the elusive confirmation that ghosts do exist.

Source Notes

Introduction: The Ghostly Relative

1. Jason Hawes and Grant Wilson with Michael Jan Friedman, *Ghost Hunting: True Stories of Unexplained Phenomena from the Atlantic Paranormal Society.* New York: Pocket Books, 2007, p. 24.
2. Hawes and Wilson, *Ghost Hunting*, p. 24.

Chapter 1: Ghost Hunter History

3. Quoted in Deborah Blum, *Ghost Hunters: William James and the Search for Scientific Proof of Life After Death.* New York: Penguin, 2006, p. 26.
4. Quoted in Troy Taylor, *The Ghost Hunter's Guidebook.* Alton, IL: Whitechapel, 2004, p. 36.
5. Taylor, *The Ghost Hunter's Guidebook*, p. 32.
6. Quoted in Laurie Sue Brockway, "An Interview with Famous 'Ghost Hunter' Hans Holzer," *OfSpirit.com.* www.ofspirit.com
7. Quoted in Jeff Belanger, "50 Years of Ghost Hunting and Research with the Warrens," Ghost Village, www.ghostvillage.com.
8. Quoted in Hawes and Wilson, *Ghost Hunting*, p. 2.

Chapter 2: What, Where, When

9. Taylor, *The Ghost Hunter's Guidebook*, p. 50.

10. Taylor, *The Ghost Hunter's Guidebook*, p. 51.
11. Quoted in Brockway, "An Interview with Famous 'Ghost Hunter' Hans Holzer."
12. Quoted in Hans Holzer, *The Ghost Hunter's Favorite Cases.* New York: Barnes and Noble, 2003, p. 568.
13. Taylor, *The Ghost Hunter's Handbook*, p. 54.
14. Hawes and Wilson, *Ghost Hunting*, p. 90.
15. Fiona Broome, "Ghosts and Ghost Hunters," Hollow Hill. http://hollowhill.com.
16. Richard Southall, *How to Be a Ghost Hunter.* St. Paul, MN: Llewellyn, 2003, p. 18.
17. Southall, *How to Be a Ghost Hunter*, p. 20.
18. Jeff Belanger, *The Ghost Files.* Franklin Lakes, NJ: New Page, 2007, p. 185.
19. Belanger, *The Ghost Files*, p. 185.
20. Grant Wilson, "Getting Started," The Atlantic Paranormal Society. www.the-atlantic-paranormal-society.com.
21. Southall, *How to Be a Ghost Hunter*, p. xxxiv.
22. Quoted in Fiona Broome, "When to Go Ghost Hunting," Hollow Hill, http://hollowhill.com.
23. Broome, "When to Go Ghost Hunting."

Chapter 3: High-Tech Ghost Hunting

24. Hawes and Wilson, *Ghost Hunting*, p. 57.

25. Quoted in Hawes and Wilson, *Ghost Hunting*, p. 58.
26. Taylor, *The Ghost Hunter's Guidebook*, p. 118.
27. Southall, *How to Be a Ghost Hunter*, p. 64.
28. Quoted in Maribeth Ward, "Hoosier State Paranormal Group Investigates Book at DePauw Library." *Banner Graphic*, January 26, 2009. www.bannergraphic.com.
29. Quoted in Ward, "Hoosier State Paranormal Group Investigates Book at DePauw Library."
30. Taylor, *The Ghost Hunter's Guidebook*, p. 123.
31. Taylor, *The Ghost Hunter's Guidebook*, p. 125.
32. Hawes and Wilson, *Ghost Hunting*, p. 212.
33. Hawes and Wilson, *Ghost Hunting*, p. 212.
34. David Betz, "The Investigator," The Atlantic Paranormal Society. www.the-atlantic-paranormal-society.com.

Chapter 4: The Hunt

35. Taylor, *The Ghost Hunter's Guidebook*, p. 140.
36. Grant Wilson, "When to Research," The Atlantic Paranormal Society." www.the-atlantic-paranormal-society.com.
37. Richard Senate, "Retrocognition at Mission La Purisima Concepcion," Ghost Village, February 18, 2009. www.ghostvillage.com.
38. Taylor, *The Ghost Hunter's Guidebook*, p. 140.
39. Holzer, *The Ghost Hunter's Favorite Cases*, p. 123.
40. Southall, *How to Be a Ghost Hunter*, p. xxiii.

41. Betz, "The Investigator."
42. Dave Juliano, "The Shadowlands University Ghost Hunting 101 Classes," Shadowlands. www.ghost-hunting101.com.
43. Wilson, "Getting Started."
44. Grant Wilson, "Give Me Some Proof: Part 1: Catching Them on Film," The Atlantic Paranormal Society. www.the-atlantic-paranormal-society.com.
45. Richard Senate, "An Active Ghost Hunt at a Haunted Bed and Breakfast," Ghost Village, July 7, 2006. www.ghostvillage.com.
46. Senate, "An Active Ghost Hunt at a Haunted Bed and Breakfast."
47. Fiona Broome, "Basic Tools Every Ghost Hunter Must Have," Hollow Hill. www.hollowhill.com.
48. Betz, "The Investigator."
49. Holzer, *The Ghost Hunter's Favorite Cases*, p. 139.
50. Al Tyas, "Keeping Emotions in Check," The Atlantic Paranormal Society. www.the-atlantic-paranormal-society.com.
51. Fiona Broome, "What to Do If a Ghost Hunt Frightens You," Hollow Hill. www.hollowhill.com.
52. Hawes and Wilson, *Ghost Hunting*, p. 126.
53. Fiona Broome, "Guidelines for Ghost Hunters," Hollow Hill. www.hollowhill.com.
54. Taylor, *The Ghost Hunter's Guidebook*, p. 17.

Chapter 5 Science or Pseudoscience?

55. Quoted in Jeff Belanger, "The Skeptic's View," Ghost Village, June 28, 2003. www.ghostvillage.com.
56. Quoted in Brian Ettkin, "Skeptic: Ghost

Hunters Practice 'Pseudoscience,'" *Albany (NY) Times-Union*, October 17, 2008. http://timesunion.com.

57. Quoted in Jeff Belanger, "The Skeptic's View."

58. Quoted in Brockway, "An Interview with Famous 'Ghost Hunter' Hans Holzer."

59. Cody Polston, "The 10 Biggest Mistakes Made by Ghost Hunters," Southwest Ghost Hunters Association. http://sgha.net.

60. Quoted in Belanger, "The Skeptic's View."

61. Alison Smith, "Gnome Hunters Skeptics and 'You People,'" Who Forted. http://whofortedblog.com.

62. Alison Smith, "Pseudoscience," *Skeptical Analysis of the Paranormal Society*. www.skepticalanalysis.com.

63. Joe Nickell, "Ghost Hunters," *Skeptical Inquirer*, September 2006. www.csicop.org.

64. Wilson, "Getting Started."

65. Belanger, *The Ghost Files*, p. 143.

66. Smith, "Pseudoscience."

67. Don Riefler, "Caution: Plumbers at Work," *SWIFT: Online Newsletter of the James Randi Educational Foundation*. www.randi.org.

68. Robert Todd Carroll, "Ghost," *The Skeptic's Dictionary*. http://skepdic.com.

69. Polston, "The 10 Biggest Mistakes Made by Ghost Hunters."

70. Quoted in Ettkin, "Skeptic: Ghost Hunters Practice 'Pseudoscience.'"

71. Polston, "The 10 Biggest Mistakes Made by Ghost Hunters."

72. Riefler, "Caution: Plumbers at Work."

73. Nickell, "Ghost Hunters."

74. Quoted in Ettkin, "Skeptic: Ghost Hunters Practice 'Pseudoscience.'"

75. Quoted in Belanger, *The Ghost Files*, p. 172.

76. Robert T. Carroll, "Ghost."

77. Quoted in Ettkin, "Skeptic: Ghost Hunters Practice 'Pseudoscience.'"

78. Alison Smith, "SAPS: Skeptical The Analysis of the Paranormal Society," Secular Student Alliance. www.secularstudents.org.

79. Alison Smith, "TAPS vs. SAPS," *eSkeptic*, August 10, 2006. www.skeptic.com.

80. Quoted in Spectral Review, "Paranormal Quotes." www.spectralreview.com.

81. Quoted in Ettkin, "Skeptic: Ghost Hunters Practice 'Pseudoscience.'"

For Further Research

Books

Jeff Belanger, *Who's Haunting the White House?* New York: Sterling, 2008.

Charles A. Coulombe, *Haunted Places in America: A Guide to Spooked and Spooky Public Places in the United States.* Guilford, CT: Lyons, 2004.

Melba Goodwyn, *Ghost Worlds: A Guide to Poltergeists, Ecto-Mist, and Spirit Behavior.* Woodbury, MN : Llewellyn, 2007.

Michael Teelbaum, *Ghosts and Real-Life Ghost Hunters.* New York: Franklin Watts, 2008.

Vince Wilson, *The Science of Ghost Hunting.* Baltimore: Cosmic Pantheon, 2008.

Web Sites

Hollow Hill: The Ghost Web site (http://hollowhill.com). Fiona Broome and her staff present dozens of articles on ghost hunting and haunted places.

National Ghost Hunters Society (www.nationalghosthunters.com). Features ghost stories, photos, an online ghost store, and a "spirit forum" for those who sign up.

SAPS: Skeptical Analysis of the Paranormal Society (www.skeptical analysis.com). Site devoted to debunking the claims of ghost hunters, mediums, and others claiming supernatural powers.

The Shadowlands: Ghosts and Hauntings (http://theshadowlands.net/ghost). Articles on ghost hunting, haunted places, and also audio and video clips of supposed paranormal events.

TAPS: The Atlantic Paranormal Society (www.the-atlantic-paranormal-society.com). The site of Jason Hawes, Grant Wilson, and their colleagues has links to dozens of articles on different aspects of ghost hunting.

Index

Rhode Island Paranormal
    Society, 19
Riefler, Don, 65, 66
Roman Catholic Church, 25
Romans, ancient, 17, 21

S

Schneider brothers, 11
science, 9–10, 64–66, 68–71
séances, 9, 56
Senate, Debbie, 54
Senate, Richard, 47–48, 54–56
sensitives, described, 18
Shakespeare, William, 23
Sheppard, Susan, 50
Sidgwick, Henry, 10
Skeptical Analysis of the
    Paranormal Society
    (SAPS), 71
Skeptical Inquirer (magazine), 61
skeptics
    arguments of, 63–64
    closed-minds of, 64
    defined, 61, 63
    Hawes and Wilson and,
        70–71
    James, William, 10
    scientific methods and,
        9–10, 65, 70
Smith, Alison, 63, 64–65, 70–71
smoking, 54
Smurl, Jack and Janet, 16–17
Society for Psychical Research
    (SPR), 10, 11
Southall, Richard
    on demons, 25
    on electronic voice
        phenomena, 36
    on entities, 24
    investigation of Mounds
        Penitentiary,
        28–29
    research by, 50
Southall, Robert, 18
spiritualism, 8–9
SS *Watertown*, 40
St. George's Hall, 57
St. Louis Cemetery (New

Orleans, Louisiana),
    29
Sylvia (ghost), 54

T

tape recorders, 35–36, 39
    (illustration)
Tarot cards, 52, 53 (illustration)
Taylor, Troy
    on characteristics needed by
        ghost hunters,
        59
    definition of ghosts, 20
    on disturbances by living
        human agents,
        23
    on electronic voice
        phenomena, 36
    on hauntings, 20, 22
    on on-site research, 48
    on orbs, 42
    on photographs, 39
    on police as information
        source, 47
    on Price, 14
telekinesis, 11
Telesco, Patricia, 31
television programs
    Ghost Hunters, 4, 19, 48,
        70–71
    Ghost Hunters International,
        48
    Ghost Man, The, 14
    popularity, 48, 61
temperature fluctuations, 34
thermal imaging cameras, 43–44
times of hauntings, 30, 31
Tinney, Edward, 28
Toronto, Canada, 30–31
Townsend, Maurice, 31
Tracy, Keith, 40
Twain, Mark, 10
two-part phenomena, 23–24
Tyas, Al, 57

U

Underwood, Peter, 14–15, 16,
    18

University of London, 11

V

video cameras, 33 (illustration)
Voices from the Universe
    (Jurgenson), 36
vortices, 40

W

Waldegrave, Henry, 13
Walls, R.D., 28–29
Warren, Ed, 16–18, 19
Warren, Lorraine, 16–17, 18, 19
Wilson, Grant
    on importance of lack of
        information
        before
        investigation, 47
    investigations by
        Canadian apartment
            building,
            30–31
        ghosts without feet,
            22–23
        Massachusetts armory,
            58–59
        Wrenn home, 4–5, 7
    on limits of science, 64
    on relying too much on
        equipment, 54
    on skeptics, 71
    skeptics' opinion of, 70–71
    on smoking, 54
    use of technology by, 19,
        33–34, 43–44
Wilson, Vince, 69–70
Wrenn family, 4–5, 7

About the Author

William W. Lace is a native of Fort Worth, Texas, where he is executive assistant to the chancellor at Tarrant County College. He holds a bachelor's degree from Texas Christian University, a master's degree from East Texas State University, and a doctorate from the University of North Texas. He has written more than 50 nonfiction books for young readers on subjects ranging from the atomic bomb to the Dallas Cowboys. He and his wife, Laura, a retired school librarian, live in Arlington, Texas, and have two children and four grandchildren.